Slash Your Bills: A Practical Guide to Saving Money in the UK

Outline and Chapters

Introduction

- The rising cost of living in the UK
- Why saving on bills matters
- The mindset shift: Small changes, big results

Chapter 1: Understanding Your Household Bills

- Breaking down common UK household expenses:
    - Energy (Gas and Electricity)
    - Water
    - Council Tax
    - Broadband and Mobile
    - Subscriptions
- How to audit your current spending

Chapter 2: Cutting Down Energy Costs

- Switching providers: How to find the best energy deals
- Understanding the Energy Price Cap
- Reducing usage:
    - Smart thermostats
    - Energy-efficient appliances
    - Simple habits (e.g., switching off standby)
- Government grants and schemes:
    - Winter Fuel Payment
    - Warm Home Discount Scheme

Chapter 3: Lowering Water Bills

- Installing a water meter: Is it right for you?
- Saving water with everyday habits
- Free water-saving gadgets from water companies
- Negotiating with your provider

Chapter 4: Reducing Council Tax

- Understanding your band and challenging it
- Council tax discounts and exemptions:
    - Single person discount
    - Disabled band reduction scheme
    - Student exemptions

Chapter 5: Cheaper Broadband and Mobile Plans

- Comparing broadband deals: What to look for
- Negotiating with your provider
- Mobile plan hacks:
    - Switching to SIM-only deals
    - Free apps to monitor usage
- Using social tariffs for low-income households

Chapter 6: Saving on Groceries

- Meal planning and shopping lists
- Best times and places for discounts in the UK
- Loyalty schemes: Tesco Clubcard, Nectar, and more
- Using apps like Too Good To Go and Olio

Chapter 7: Cutting Down Subscription Costs

- Reviewing and cancelling unused subscriptions
- Sharing and family plans
- Alternatives to paid services (e.g., library memberships)

Chapter 8: Transport Savings

- Using public transport discounts:
    - Railcards
    - Bus passes
- Car ownership costs:
    - How to lower insurance premiums
    - Switching to fuel-efficient driving habits
- Cycling and walking as alternatives

Chapter 9: Debt Management and Financial Support

- Reducing interest on credit cards and loans
- Accessing free financial advice in the UK
    - Citizens Advice
    - StepChange Debt Charity
- Understanding benefits and government support schemes

Chapter 10: Long-Term Savings Strategies

- Switching banks for cashback and rewards
- Building an emergency fund
- Investing in energy-saving home improvements:
    - Insulation
    - Solar panels

Chapter 11: Free Resources and Tools

- Websites and apps for comparison shopping:
    - MoneySavingExpert
    - Uswitch
    - ComparetheMarket
- Free budgeting tools and apps
- Community support: Facebook groups, forums, and local initiatives

---

Conclusion

- Celebrating small wins
- How to stay motivated and consistent
- The power of sharing tips with others

Bonus Content

- Printable monthly bill tracker
- Top UK websites and resources for saving money
- Checklist: Quick wins to save on your bills today

Chapter 1: Understanding Your Household Bills

Household bills are a significant portion of every UK resident's monthly expenses. By understanding what you're paying for and how costs are calculated, you can identify opportunities to reduce your outgoings. In this chapter, we'll break down the main types of household bills and guide you on how to audit your current spending effectively.

The Main Household Bills in the UK

1. **Energy (Gas and Electricity)**
   - **What You're Paying For**: Your energy bill consists of usage charges (based on the amount of gas and electricity consumed) and a standing charge (a daily fee to keep you connected to the energy network).
   - **Factors Influencing Costs**:
     - Energy price cap changes
     - Type of tariff (fixed vs. variable)
     - Seasonal fluctuations (higher costs in winter)

- **Common Mistakes**:
    - Staying on a standard tariff after your fixed deal ends
    - Ignoring energy-efficient habits

2. **Water**
    - **What You're Paying For**: Water charges cover supply (clean water to your home) and wastewater (removal and treatment of sewage).
    - **Billing Methods**:
        - **Metered**: Charged based on usage.
        - **Unmetered**: A fixed amount based on your property's "rateable value."
    - **Common Mistakes**:
        - Not considering switching to a water meter if you live alone or in a small household.
        - Overlooking free water-saving devices offered by water companies.

3. **Council Tax**
    - **What You're Paying For**: Council tax funds local services such as waste collection, road maintenance, and schools.

- **How It's Calculated**:
    - Based on your property's band (A-H) in England and Scotland, with slight variations in Wales and Northern Ireland.
- **Common Mistakes**:
    - Paying the full amount without checking for discounts or exemptions.
    - Not challenging an incorrect band valuation.

4. **Broadband and Mobile**
    - **What You're Paying For**:
    Monthly charges for internet services and mobile phone plans, often including data, calls, and texts.
    - **Common Mistakes**:
        - Letting contracts roll over to higher tariffs after the introductory period.
        - Paying for features you don't use, like unlimited data or premium TV bundles.

5. **Subscriptions**
   - **What You're Paying For:** Entertainment (Netflix, Spotify), cloud storage, gym memberships, and other recurring services.
   - **Common Mistakes:**
     - Forgetting to cancel unused subscriptions.
     - Paying full price instead of leveraging family or student discounts.

How to Audit Your Bills

Performing a household bill audit is the first step in identifying areas where you can cut costs. Here's how to do it:

1. **Gather All Your Bills**
   - Print or download your most recent bills for gas, electricity, water, council tax, broadband, and any subscriptions.
   - Use a spreadsheet or budgeting app to list each bill, its amount, and due date.

2. **Break Down Each Bill**
    - Identify standing charges versus usage charges.
    - Note any penalties, late fees, or additional services you might be paying for.
3. **Compare Your Spending to Averages**
    - Use resources like *MoneySavingExpert* or *Ofgem* to see how your bills compare to UK averages:
        - Average energy bill (2024): ~£2,000/year.
        - Average broadband cost: £30-£40/month.
        - Average council tax (Band D): ~£1,500/year.
4. **Look for Red Flags**
    - Are you consistently paying more than average?
    - Have your bills increased recently without explanation?
    - Are you on a standard tariff for energy or broadband?
5. **Highlight Areas for Savings**
    - Prioritise bills that can be renegotiated or reduced quickly, such as energy tariffs, broadband contracts, and subscriptions.

Spotlight: Tools to Track Your Bills

- **Apps:**
    - **Money Dashboard:** Links your bank accounts and categorises spending.
    - **Emma:** Identifies unused subscriptions and tracks expenses.
    - **Cleo:** Provides bill insights and saving tips.
- **Websites:**
    - **Uswitch:** Compares energy, broadband, and mobile tariffs.
    - **Compare the Market:** Includes household bills, insurance, and more.
    - **Council Tax Refund Checker:** Helps you check for overpayment or incorrect bands.

Quick Wins for the Time-Poor

If you don't have time to dive into a detailed audit, start with these steps:

1. Switch to online billing to avoid paper charges.
2. Set up Direct Debits to avoid late payment fees.
3. Use comparison sites to check if you're overpaying on energy, broadband, or mobile services.

Conclusion

Understanding your household bills is the foundation for cutting costs. Once you know what you're paying for, you can confidently move on to strategies for reducing these expenses in the following chapters. Every pound saved here is a step closer to financial freedom.

Chapter 2: Cutting Down Energy Costs

Energy bills are one of the most significant expenses for households in the UK, especially during the winter months. With the energy price cap fluctuating and increasing demand for power, finding ways to reduce these costs can make a substantial difference. In this chapter, we'll explore practical strategies to lower your energy bills without sacrificing comfort.

Understanding Your Energy Bill

Before making changes, it's crucial to understand how your energy provider calculates your bill:

1. **Usage Charges**
   - Based on the amount of gas and electricity you consume, measured in kilowatt-hours (kWh).
   - Usage charges fluctuate with energy market prices.
2. **Standing Charges**
   - A daily fee to cover the cost of maintaining your connection to the grid and administrative expenses.
   - These are fixed and charged regardless of how much energy you use.

3. **Taxes and Levies**
   - Bills include VAT (set at 5% for domestic energy) and environmental levies.

Switching Providers: The Quickest Way to Save

Switching energy providers or tariffs can save you hundreds of pounds annually.

1. **Comparison Sites**
   - Use websites like *Uswitch*, *MoneySuperMarket*, or *Compare the Market* to find the best deals.
   - Check for both fixed-rate and variable-rate tariffs.
2. **When to Switch**
   - If your fixed tariff is ending, switch to avoid being moved to a standard variable rate.
   - Use reminders or apps to track contract end dates.

3. **Green Tariffs**
   - Many green tariffs are now competitive in price. Providers like Octopus Energy and Bulb offer renewable energy at affordable rates.

Simple Habits to Reduce Usage

Small changes in daily habits can lead to big savings:

1. **Heating and Hot Water**
   - Set your thermostat 1°C lower. This can save up to £80 per year.
   - Only heat the rooms you use with radiator controls.
   - Insulate your hot water tank with a jacket (saves around £50 annually).
2. **Lighting**
   - Switch to LED bulbs, which use 75% less energy than traditional bulbs.
   - Turn off lights when leaving a room.
3. **Appliances**
   - Avoid using standby mode. Turning devices off at the plug can save £30 a year.

- Run dishwashers and washing machines on eco modes and only with full loads.

4. **Cooking**
   - Use lids on pots and pans to reduce cooking times.
   - Boil only the amount of water you need in your kettle.

Investing in Energy Efficiency

While some measures require upfront costs, they provide long-term savings:

1. **Smart Thermostats**
   - Devices like Hive or Nest can optimise your heating schedule and reduce waste. Savings: £100-£150 per year.
2. **Loft and Wall Insulation**
   - Proper insulation can reduce heating costs by 25%.
   - Check for government grants under the ECO scheme or local council programs.

3. **Double Glazing**
   - Upgrading single-glazed windows reduces heat loss and external noise.
4. **Solar Panels**
   - Though costly upfront, solar panels can cut energy bills by 30-50%. Some councils offer financial assistance or interest-free loans.

Government Schemes and Grants

The UK government provides financial support to help households manage energy costs:

1. **Energy Price Cap**
   - Regulated by Ofgem, the cap limits what suppliers can charge on standard tariffs.
   - Stay informed about cap changes to adjust your usage accordingly.
2. **Warm Home Discount Scheme**
   - A £150 rebate for eligible low-income households. Check with your provider to see if you qualify.

3. **Winter Fuel Payment**
   - A tax-free payment for pensioners, ranging from £100 to £300.
4. **ECO4 Scheme**
   - Offers free or subsidised energy efficiency improvements like insulation and heating system upgrades.

Using Smart Technology

Smart devices help monitor and reduce energy usage:

1. **Smart Meters**
   - Installed free by your energy supplier.
   - Displays real-time usage, helping you identify energy-wasting habits.
2. **Energy Monitoring Apps**
   - Apps like Loop and Samsung SmartThings Energy track your usage and suggest ways to cut costs.

Quick Wins for Reducing Energy Bills

1. Use draft excluders on doors and windows.
2. Wash clothes at 30°C instead of 40°C.
3. Bleed your radiators regularly to ensure efficiency.
4. Take shorter showers or install an energy-efficient showerhead.
5. Switch to off-peak tariffs if you can shift usage to evenings or weekends.

Case Study: Jane's £400 Annual Energy Saving

Jane, a single mother in Manchester, reduced her energy bills significantly by:

1. Switching from a standard tariff to a fixed-rate deal, saving £200 annually.
2. Installing LED bulbs throughout her home, cutting lighting costs by £50.
3. Using a smart thermostat to optimise heating schedules, saving £150.

Conclusion

Cutting energy costs doesn't have to mean living in discomfort. By making smarter choices, adopting energy-saving habits, and taking advantage of government schemes, you can significantly reduce your bills while contributing to a greener planet. In the next chapter, we'll look at how to tackle water bills and make savings without turning off the tap.

Chapter 3: Lowering Water Bills

Water is a vital utility, but many UK households overpay due to inefficient usage or unoptimised billing methods. Fortunately, water bills offer several opportunities for savings. In this chapter, we'll explore ways to lower your water expenses while adopting sustainable practices that benefit both your wallet and the environment.

Understanding Your Water Bill

Your water bill typically includes two main charges:

1. **Water Supply**
    - This covers the cost of clean water delivered to your home for drinking, cooking, and cleaning.
2. **Sewerage (Wastewater)**
    - This charge includes the cost of removing and treating the water that goes down your drains.

Metered vs. Unmetered Billing

Unmetered Billing

- Based on your property's rateable value (set in the 1970s).
- You pay a fixed amount regardless of how much water you use.

Metered Billing

- Charges are based on the amount of water you use (measured in cubic meters).
- Generally cheaper for smaller households or low water users.

Key Tip: If you live alone or in a small household, switching to a water meter could save you up to £100 per year. Many water companies offer a free trial period, allowing you to switch back if it doesn't reduce your costs.

Ways to Reduce Water Usage

1. In the Bathroom

- **Shorten Showers**: Reducing shower time by just one minute can save 2,500 litres of water annually.
- **Install a Water-Saving Showerhead**: These reduce flow without sacrificing pressure, saving up to £20 a year.
- **Fix Leaky Taps**: A dripping tap can waste over 5,000 litres annually.
- **Dual-Flush Toilets**: Use the smaller flush button for liquid waste, reducing water usage per flush by 50%.

2. In the Kitchen

- **Only Run Full Loads**: Use dishwashers and washing machines only when full to save water and energy.
- **Handwashing Dishes**: Use a bowl instead of running water to save up to 50% of water used.
- **Don't Overfill the Kettle**: Boil only the amount you need to save water and energy.

3. In the Garden

- **Use a Water Butt**: Collect rainwater to water plants instead of using a hosepipe.
- **Water Plants in the Morning or Evening**: Reduces evaporation, making watering more efficient.
- **Choose Drought-Resistant Plants**: Require less frequent watering.

Free Water-Saving Devices

Most UK water companies offer free gadgets to help you save water. These include:

1. **Tap Aerators**: Mix air with water to reduce flow without losing pressure.
2. **Shower Timers**: Encourage shorter showers.
3. **Cistern Bags**: Displace water in your toilet tank, reducing the amount used per flush.

Visit your water provider's website to order these free tools.

Negotiating with Your Water Provider

Unlike energy, you can't switch water providers in the UK, but you can still reduce your bill:

1. **Ask About Social Tariffs**
   - Many water companies offer discounted rates for low-income households.
   - Eligibility is based on income or specific benefits like Universal Credit.
2. **Cap Your Sewerage Charges**
   - If you use minimal water outside (e.g., no garden hose or car washing), ask your provider to cap your sewerage charges.
3. **Request a Review of Your Bill**
   - If your usage has decreased (e.g., fewer people in the household), your bill may need adjusting.

Government Schemes and Support

WaterSure Scheme

This scheme caps water bills for households that:

- Are on a meter.
- Receive certain benefits.
- Use high amounts of water due to medical conditions or having three or more children.

Hardship Funds

If you're struggling to pay your water bills, many providers offer hardship funds or payment plans. Contact your water company to explore options.

Case Study: Mark's Water Bill Success

Mark, a family man in Birmingham, reduced his water bill by £180 a year:

1. **Switched to a Meter**: Realised his family of three didn't use enough water to justify unmetered billing.

2. **Installed Free Water-Saving Devices**: Reduced water usage without noticeable lifestyle changes.
3. **Watered Garden with Rainwater**: Installed a water butt to collect rainwater for free.

Quick Wins for Saving Water

1. Turn off the tap while brushing your teeth to save 6 litres per minute.
2. Use leftover cooking water to water plants.
3. Wash your car using a bucket and sponge instead of a hose.

Conclusion

Lowering your water bill is achievable through small adjustments, efficient tools, and exploring the right billing option. The savings can quickly add up, helping you cut costs while contributing to water conservation efforts. In the next chapter, we'll tackle council tax, offering tips to reduce one of the most significant household expenses.

Chapter 4: Reducing Council Tax

Council tax is one of the largest regular expenses for households in the UK, yet many people are unaware of how to reduce their payments or whether they're even paying the correct amount. In this chapter, we'll guide you through understanding your council tax bill, identifying potential savings, and taking action to reduce your costs.

Understanding Council Tax

1. **What is Council Tax?**
    - Council tax is a local tax charged on residential properties to fund essential local services such as waste collection, schools, libraries, and police services.
2. **How is it Calculated?**
    - Each property is assigned a **band** (A-H in England and Scotland, A-I in Wales) based on its value as of April 1991.
    - The amount you pay depends on your band and the rates set by your local council.

3. **Components of Council Tax**:
   - A fixed portion goes to your local council.
   - Contributions may also go to fire services, police, and other authorities.

Check Your Council Tax Band

Many UK households are in the wrong band and could be overpaying. Here's how to check:

1. **Find Your Band**:
   - Visit the *Valuation Office Agency (VOA)* for England or the *Scottish Assessors Association* for Scotland.
   - Enter your postcode to find your property's band.
2. **Compare with Neighbours**:
   - Check the bands of similar properties on your street. If yours is higher, you might be overpaying.
3. **Challenge Your Band**:
   - Gather evidence, such as property valuations or neighbouring bands.
   - Contact your local Valuation Office to request a reassessment.

- Note: Only challenge if you're confident, as your band could increase!

Claiming Discounts and Exemptions

Depending on your circumstances, you may be eligible for a council tax reduction. Here are the main categories:

1. Single Person Discount

- A 25% discount is available if you live alone or are the only adult in the property.

2. Students

- Full-time students are exempt from council tax. If you share a house, the property may also be exempt.

3. Low-Income Households

- If you're on a low income or receiving benefits, you may qualify for a **Council Tax Reduction (CTR)**.
- Apply through your local council's website.

4. Disabled Band Reduction Scheme

- If your property has been adapted for a disabled resident, you may qualify for a reduction to the next lowest band.

5. Other Exemptions

- Properties left empty by someone in care or hospital.
- Homes occupied only by under-18s.
- Armed forces accommodation.

Appealing Additional Charges

If you've been charged extra for specific services, such as waste collection or garden maintenance, you can:

- Review your bill to understand what's included.
- Contact your local council to dispute or adjust these charges if you believe they are incorrect.

Saving on Council Tax for Empty Properties

If you own an empty property, you may be eligible for:

1. **Exemptions**: Certain empty properties (e.g., awaiting probate) are exempt from council tax.
2. **Discounts**: Some councils offer reduced rates for properties that are unfurnished or undergoing significant renovations.

Ways to Spread Payments

1. **Switch to 12-Month Payments**:
    - Most councils divide council tax over 10 months, leaving two months without payments.
    - Requesting a 12-month payment plan reduces the monthly amount, easing cash flow.
2. **Direct Debit Discounts**:
    - Some councils offer small discounts for paying via direct debit.

3. **Payment Plans**:
   - If you're struggling to pay, contact your council to arrange a manageable plan.

Case Study: Sarah's Council Tax Savings

Sarah, a single professional living in London, saved £450 a year by:

1. **Challenging her Band**: Found her house was incorrectly categorised compared to neighbours.
2. **Claiming the Single Person Discount**: Reduced her bill by 25%.
3. **Switching to a 12-Month Payment Plan**: Smoothed out her payments over the year.

Tools to Help Manage Council Tax

1. **Council Websites**:
   - Use your local council's website to check your bill, apply for discounts, or set up payments.
   -

2. **Online Calculators**:
    - Tools like *MoneySavingExpert's Council Tax Checker* can help identify potential savings.
3. **VOA Resources**:
    - Use the Valuation Office Agency site to gather evidence for challenging your band.

Quick Wins for Reducing Council Tax

1. Check your band and challenge it if necessary.
2. Apply for all eligible discounts (e.g., single person, student exemptions).
3. Switch to a 12-month payment plan to reduce monthly outgoings.

Conclusion

Reducing council tax may require a bit of effort, but the potential savings make it worthwhile. From ensuring you're in the correct band to claiming discounts, these steps can significantly lower this unavoidable expense

Chapter 5: Cheaper Broadband and Mobile Plans

Broadband and mobile bills are essential in today's connected world, but many UK households overpay by sticking with outdated contracts or failing to shop around for better deals. This chapter will guide you through saving money on these services without sacrificing quality.

Understanding Your Broadband and Mobile Costs

1. **Broadband Costs**
    - Monthly charges typically include line rental, data allowance, and additional services like TV packages.
    - Average broadband costs in the UK are £30-£40 per month, but prices vary based on speed, provider, and location.
2. **Mobile Costs**
    - Mobile plans include a combination of minutes, texts, and data.
    - Contracts often bundle the cost of a handset with service charges, leading to higher monthly payments.

How to Save on Broadband

1. Compare Deals Regularly

- Use comparison websites like *Uswitch*, *Compare the Market*, or *Broadband Genie* to find better deals.
- Check for cashback offers or vouchers when switching providers.

2. Negotiate with Your Current Provider

- If you're happy with your service but not the price, call your provider and ask for a better deal. Mention cheaper competitors as leverage.
- Providers often have retention offers to keep existing customers.

3. Bundle Services

- Combining broadband, TV, and phone services can save money.
- Providers like Sky, Virgin Media, and BT offer discounts for bundling.

4. Downgrade Your Speed

- Assess your actual needs. If you don't stream in 4K or game online, a lower-speed package might suffice.
- For basic usage (browsing, emails), speeds of 30-50 Mbps are usually adequate.

5. Avoid Unnecessary Add-Ons

- Remove optional extras like landline calls if you rarely use them.
- Check if you're paying for additional services like antivirus or cloud storage that you don't need.

6. Social Tariffs for Low-Income Households

- Many providers offer discounted broadband plans for those on benefits such as Universal Credit.
- Examples include BT's Home Essentials and Virgin Media's Essential Broadband.

How to Save on Mobile Plans

1. Switch to SIM-Only Deals

- Once your contract ends, switch to a SIM-only deal if your handset is still in good condition. These plans are significantly cheaper.
- Providers like Giffgaff, Smarty, and Voxi offer flexible SIM-only deals starting from £6/month.

2. Avoid Overpaying for Data

- Check your actual data usage. Many people overpay for unlimited data plans they don't need.
- Downgrade to a lower data plan if your usage is modest (e.g., less than 5GB/month).

3. Use Pay-As-You-Go Plans

- If you use your phone minimally, consider pay-as-you-go. This option can save money compared to monthly plans.

4. Family or Group Plans

- Family bundles allow multiple users to share data, minutes, and texts, often at a discount.
- Providers like EE, Vodafone, and O2 offer shared plans.

5. Check for Discounts

- Students and NHS staff can access special discounts on mobile plans.
- Some companies, like Vodafone and Three, offer loyalty rewards or discounts for long-term customers.

Tips for Negotiating Better Deals

1. **Know Your Options**
   - Research competitors' prices before calling your current provider. Mentioning a rival's cheaper offer can strengthen your position.
2. **Call When Your Contract Ends**
   - Providers often hike prices after your initial contract period. Use this opportunity to negotiate or switch.

3. **Be Willing to Leave**
   - Providers often offer discounts or perks to customers who say they're leaving.

Case Study: David's £300 Savings

David, a small business owner in Manchester, saved over £300 a year by:

1. **Switching Broadband Providers**: He moved from BT to Vodafone, reducing his monthly bill by £15 while maintaining similar speeds.
2. **Choosing a SIM-Only Deal**: After his phone contract ended, he switched to Smarty, cutting his mobile bill in half.
3. **Negotiating Add-Ons**: He removed an unused TV package, saving an extra £10/month.

Tools to Help Save on Broadband and Mobile

1. **Comparison Websites**
   - *Uswitch, Broadband Genie*, and *MoneySuperMarket* provide updated deals.
2. **Mobile Monitoring Apps**
   - Apps like *My Data Manager* help track data usage, so you don't overpay for unused data.
3. **Speed Test Tools**
   - Use tools like *Ookla Speedtest* to ensure you're getting the speeds you're paying for.

Quick Wins for Reducing Broadband and Mobile Bills

1. Switch to a SIM-only deal after your handset is paid off.
2. Use public Wi-Fi where possible to save mobile data.
3. Downgrade your broadband package if you're not using high-speed services.
4. Consolidate family plans for better discounts.

Conclusion

Broadband and mobile bills often go unnoticed but can account for a significant portion of household expenses. By regularly reviewing your contracts, negotiating with providers, and avoiding unnecessary extras, you can save hundreds of pounds annually. In the next chapter, we'll explore strategies for saving money on groceries, another major area where UK households often overspend.

Chapter 6: Saving on Groceries

Groceries are one of the biggest recurring expenses for UK households, and rising food prices have made it even more challenging to stay within budget. However, with strategic planning and smart shopping techniques, you can significantly cut down on your grocery bill without compromising on quality or nutrition. This chapter will provide practical tips and resources to help you save money on food and household essentials.

Understanding Your Grocery Spending

Before making changes, it's important to assess your current habits:

1. **Track Your Spending**
    - Keep receipts for a month and categorise your purchases (e.g., fresh produce, snacks, household items).
    - Use apps like *Emma* or *Money Dashboard* to track and analyse grocery spending.

2. **Identify Wastage**
   - Are you throwing away food regularly?
   - Focus on reducing waste to maximise the value of what you buy.

Smart Shopping Tips

1. Plan Your Meals

- Create a weekly meal plan to avoid impulse buying and reduce waste.
- Base your plan on what's already in your fridge, freezer, and pantry.

2. Write a Shopping List

- Stick to your list when shopping to avoid unnecessary purchases.
- Use apps like *Bring!* or *Out of Milk* to organise your list efficiently.

3. Shop at Budget-Friendly Stores

- Discount supermarkets like Aldi and Lidl often offer significant savings compared to premium chains like Waitrose.

- Look for own-brand products, which are often just as good as branded items but cost much less.

4. Use Loyalty Cards

- Sign up for loyalty programs like:
    - Tesco Clubcard: Access exclusive discounts and earn points.
    - Sainsbury's Nectar: Collect points for money off future purchases.
    - Boots Advantage Card: Save on health and beauty products.

5. Shop Online

- Shopping online can help you stick to your budget by avoiding in-store temptations.
- Use price comparison tools like *Trolley.co.uk* to find the cheapest options across multiple supermarkets.

Timing is Everything

1. Shop at the Right Time

- Visit stores in the evening to find markdowns on fresh produce, meat, and bakery items.
- Look for yellow sticker discounts in supermarkets like Tesco and Asda.

2. Stock Up During Sales

- Take advantage of "buy one, get one free" offers and bulk deals, but only for items you use regularly.
- Check weekly ads for discounts and promotions.

Cutting Costs on Specific Items

1. Fresh Produce

- Buy seasonal fruits and vegetables, which are cheaper and fresher.
- Visit local markets for better deals on produce.

2. Meat and Fish

- Buy larger cuts of meat and portion them yourself.
- Use alternatives like beans and lentils to stretch meals.
- Look for frozen fish, which is often cheaper than fresh.

3. Household Items

- Stock up on essentials like toilet paper and cleaning products during sales.
- Try budget-friendly brands for non-food items.

Reduce Food Waste

1. **Store Food Properly**
    - Use airtight containers to keep food fresh longer.
    - Learn the difference between "use by" and "best before" dates.
2. **Repurpose Leftovers**
    - Transform leftovers into new meals (e.g., roasted chicken into soup or curry).

- Freeze unused portions for future use.
3. **Use Food-Waste Apps**
    - Apps like *Too Good To Go* and *Olio* let you buy surplus food at a discount or even get it for free.

Take Advantage of Cashback Apps

Earn cashback on groceries with apps like:

1. **Shopmium**: Get cashback on selected items, often making them free.
2. **CheckoutSmart**: Offers rewards for buying specific products.
3. **GreenJinn**: Focuses on healthy and eco-friendly grocery options.

Case Study: Emily's Grocery Savings

Emily, a mother of two in Manchester, reduced her grocery bill by £200 per month by:

1. **Meal Planning**: Created weekly menus based on items already in her pantry.
2. **Shopping at Aldi**: Switched from a premium supermarket, cutting costs on staples.
3. **Using Cashback Apps**: Earned £30 per month using *Shopmium* and *CheckoutSmart*.
4. **Reducing Food Waste**: Froze leftovers and repurposed meals.

Tools and Resources for Grocery Savings

1. **Meal Planning Apps**: *Mealime*, *Yummly*
2. **Budget Trackers**: *Money Dashboard*, *Goodbudget*
3. **Comparison Sites**: *Trolley.co.uk*, *mysupermarket.co.uk*

Quick Wins for Saving on Groceries

1. Shop with a list and stick to it.
2. Cook in bulk and freeze portions for later.
3. Buy own-brand or discounted products instead of premium brands.
4. Use loyalty cards and cashback apps to maximise savings.

Conclusion

Saving on groceries is a combination of smart shopping, planning, and reducing waste. By making small, consistent changes to your habits, you can significantly lower your grocery expenses while maintaining a healthy and balanced diet.

Chapter 7: Cutting Down Subscription Costs

In today's digital age, subscription services are everywhere—streaming platforms, fitness apps, software, and more. While convenient, they can quickly add up and eat into your budget. Many households unknowingly pay for services they no longer use or could easily replace with free alternatives. This chapter will help you identify, manage, and reduce your subscription expenses.

Step 1: Audit Your Subscriptions

1. **List All Active Subscriptions**
    - Review your bank statements or use apps like *Emma*, *Cleo*, or *Snoop* to identify recurring payments.
    - Common categories include:
        - Streaming services (Netflix, Disney+, Amazon Prime)
        - Music apps (Spotify, Apple Music)
        - Cloud storage (Google Drive, Dropbox)
        - Fitness apps or gym memberships
        - Subscription boxes (food, beauty, or hobbies)

2. **Assess Usage**
   - Ask yourself:
     - How often do I use this service?
     - Is there a free or cheaper alternative?
     - Could I share the cost with someone else?

Step 2: Cancel or Pause Unused Subscriptions

1. **Cancel Unused Services**
   - If you haven't used a subscription in the last month, it's a good candidate for cancellation.
   - Many services allow you to cancel online quickly; some may even offer discounts to retain you.
2. **Pause Seasonal Subscriptions**
   - Some services, like fitness apps or TV streaming platforms, allow you to pause rather than cancel.
   - This is particularly useful for services you use only part of the year.

Step 3: Negotiate for Lower Prices

1. **Call Customer Support**
   - Providers often offer discounts or incentives to keep you as a customer.
   - Mention cheaper competitor services during the call.
2. **Leverage Free Trials**
   - Many platforms offer free trials or introductory offers.
   - Rotate between services to take advantage of these deals but remember to cancel before the trial ends.
3. **Ask for Loyalty Discounts**
   - If you've been a long-term customer, ask for a reduced rate or extra perks.

Step 4: Share or Bundle Subscriptions

1. **Family Plans**
    - Many services offer shared plans for multiple users:
        - Spotify and Apple Music Family Plans
        - Netflix Standard or Premium Plans
    - Sharing reduces the per-person cost significantly.
2. **Split Costs with Friends or Family**
    - Services like *Spliiit* help you securely share subscriptions and split costs.
3. **Bundle Deals**
    - Providers like Amazon (Prime Video + delivery benefits) or Apple (Apple One) combine multiple services into a discounted package.

Step 5: Replace Paid Services with Free Alternatives

1. **Streaming and Entertainment**
   - Use free platforms like *BBC iPlayer*, *All 4*, and *YouTube*.
   - Explore free audiobooks from *Libby* or *BorrowBox* via your local library.
2. **Fitness and Wellness Apps**
   - Switch to free fitness resources on YouTube or apps like *FitOn*.
3. **Cloud Storage**
   - Use free tiers of Google Drive, OneDrive, or Dropbox for small storage needs.
4. **News and Magazines**
   - Replace paid subscriptions with free news apps like *BBC News* or *Flipboard*.

Step 6: Keep Subscriptions in Check

1. **Set Alerts for Renewal Dates**
   - Use a calendar or app to track renewal dates and cancel before automatic renewals if needed.
   - Many apps offer notifications for upcoming payments.

2. **Limit Subscriptions**
   - Stick to a set number of subscriptions at any given time. Cancel one before adding another.
3. **Evaluate Monthly**
   - Review your subscriptions regularly to ensure you're getting value from each one.

Case Study: Sarah's Subscription Overhaul

Sarah, a graphic designer in Leeds, was spending £90/month on subscriptions. Here's how she reduced her costs:

1. **Cancelled Unused Services**: Stopped paying for a fitness app and two streaming platforms she rarely used, saving £40/month.
2. **Switched to a Family Plan**: Joined a shared Spotify plan with friends, cutting her music costs by £7/month.
3. **Used Free Alternatives**: Replaced paid fitness apps with YouTube workouts.

Total Savings: £60/month or £720/year.

Quick Wins for Subscription Savings

1. Cancel subscriptions you haven't used in the past month.
2. Switch to family or shared plans to reduce individual costs.
3. Use free trials strategically and set reminders to cancel before renewal.
4. Consolidate subscriptions into bundles for better value.

Tools to Manage Subscriptions

1. **Apps**:
    - *Emma*: Tracks and highlights recurring payments.
    - *Cleo*: Helps you identify unnecessary expenses.
2. **Websites**:
    - *MoneySavingExpert.com*: Offers deals and discounts for popular services.

Conclusion

Subscriptions can silently drain your budget, but with a proactive approach, you can take control of these expenses. By auditing your subscriptions, cancelling unused services, and leveraging discounts or free alternatives, you can enjoy the benefits of these services without overspending. In the next chapter, we'll tackle transport costs and how to save on travel and commuting in the UK.

Chapter 8: Transport Savings

Transport is another significant expense for UK households, whether you're commuting to work, running errands, or taking occasional trips. Fuel prices, insurance premiums, and public transport fares can quickly add up, but there are many ways to save. This chapter explores practical strategies to reduce your transport costs without compromising convenience.

Understanding Transport Costs

Your transport expenses likely fall into these categories:

1. **Public Transport**
    - Train, bus, and underground fares.
2. **Private Vehicle Costs**
    - Fuel, insurance, maintenance, road tax, and parking fees.
3. **Alternative Transport**
    - Cycling, walking, car-sharing, and other eco-friendly options.

Saving on Public Transport

1. Use Railcards

- Railcards offer up to **1/3 off train fares** and typically cost £30/year. Options include:
    - **16-25 Railcard**: For young adults and students.
    - **26-30 Railcard**: For young professionals.
    - **Two Together Railcard**: For pairs traveling together.
    - **Family & Friends Railcard**: For groups with children.
    - **Senior Railcard**: For travellers aged 60+.

2. Take Advantage of Travel Passes

- Save on daily commutes with passes like:
    - **Oyster Cards**: Discounted fares for London travel.
    - **Weekly or Monthly Travelcards**: Cost-effective for regular journeys.
    - **Bus Season Tickets**: Offered by local bus services, such as Stagecoach or Arriva.

3. Book in Advance

- Advance train tickets are significantly cheaper than on-the-day purchases. Use apps like *Trainline* or *National Rail* to book early.

4. Travel Off-Peak

- Travel during off-peak hours to save on train, tube, and bus fares. Check your provider's website for specific off-peak times.

5. Explore Discounts

- Many councils and transport operators offer discounts for:
    - Students
    - Apprentices
    - Low-income households (e.g., Travel Discount Cards)

Saving on Private Vehicle Costs

1. Reduce Fuel Costs

- **Drive Smarter**: Reduce fuel consumption by:
    - Accelerating gradually.
    - Avoiding heavy braking.
    - Maintaining a steady speed.
- **Use Fuel Price Comparison Tools**:
    - Apps like *PetrolPrices* and *Confused.com* find the cheapest fuel near you.
- **Avoid Overloading**: Remove unnecessary items from your car to improve fuel efficiency.

2. Lower Insurance Premiums

- Shop around for the best deals using comparison sites like *Compare the Market*, *GoCompare*, and *MoneySuperMarket*.
- Increase your voluntary excess to lower premiums.
- Use a black box policy if you're a safe driver.

3. Cut Maintenance Costs

- Perform basic maintenance yourself, such as checking oil and tire pressure.
- Use local garages instead of dealerships for servicing.
- Look for deals on MOTs and routine checks.

4. Share Rides

- Carpool with colleagues or friends to split fuel and parking costs.
- Use car-sharing platforms like *Liftshare* or *BlaBlaCar*.

Consider Alternative Transport Options

1. Cycling

- Cycling is a cost-effective and eco-friendly way to travel.
- Use government schemes like **Cycle to Work**, which allows you to purchase a bike tax-free, saving up to 42%.

2. Walking

- For short distances, walking is the cheapest option.
- Track your steps with fitness apps to stay motivated and healthy.

3. E-Scooters

- In some cities, renting e-scooters can be a cheaper alternative for short journeys. Providers like *Voi* and *Lime* offer pay-as-you-go options.

Saving on Parking

1. Use Parking Apps

- Apps like *JustPark*, *YourParkingSpace*, and *Parkopedia* help you find cheaper parking spots or book in advance.

2. Avoid City Centres

- Park slightly outside the city and walk or take public transport the rest of the way.

3. Apply for Resident Permits

- If you live in an area with controlled parking, apply for a resident permit, which is often cheaper than daily parking fees.

Government Schemes and Discounts

1. **Bus Pass for Free Travel**
   - Seniors and disabled people can apply for free bus travel through local councils.
2. **Low Emission Zones (LEZs)**
   - Avoid charges in cities like London by driving low-emission or electric vehicles.
3. **Electric Vehicle Grants**
   - The UK government offers grants for purchasing electric vehicles or installing home charging points.

Case Study: Tom's Transport Savings

Tom, a teacher in Birmingham, reduced his annual transport costs by £700 by:

1. **Switching to a Railcard**: Saved 1/3 on train fares for his daily commute.
2. **Carpooling**: Shared rides with colleagues twice a week, halving his fuel expenses.
3. **Using Parking Apps**: Booked cheaper parking spots in advance, saving £10 per week.

Tools for Transport Savings

1. **Comparison Sites**: *Trainline, PetrolPrices, Confused.com.*
2. **Transport Apps**: *Citymapper, Uber, JustPark.*
3. **Cycling Resources**: *Sustrans* (cycling routes and tips).

Quick Wins for Transport Savings

1. Use railcards or travel passes for regular journeys.
2. Compare and switch car insurance providers annually.
3. Carpool or use alternative transport to cut costs.
4. Drive more efficiently to save on fuel.

Conclusion

Transport costs can quickly spiral out of control, but with careful planning and resourceful choices, you can make significant savings. By optimising your public transport habits, reducing vehicle expenses, and exploring alternatives like cycling or walking, you can keep your travel costs manageable. In the next chapter, we'll discuss long-term savings strategies to help you build financial resilience and reduce your overall expenses.

Chapter 9: Long-Term Savings Strategies

While immediate cost-cutting measures are essential, developing long-term savings strategies will help you build financial resilience and reduce overall expenses over time. In this chapter, we'll explore actionable steps you can take to lower your household costs sustainably, maximise your savings, and achieve greater financial security.

1. Invest in Energy Efficiency

Energy-efficient upgrades can result in significant savings on your utility bills over time. Consider these options:

1.1. Home Insulation

- Properly insulating your home can reduce heat loss and cut heating costs by up to 25%.
- Focus on loft, cavity wall, and solid wall insulation.
- Check if you're eligible for government schemes like the **ECO4 Grant** to cover some or all of the costs.

1.2. Energy-Efficient Appliances

- When replacing appliances, look for energy-efficient models rated A+++ or higher.
- Though they may cost more upfront, they save money on electricity and water bills in the long run.

1.3. Renewable Energy

- Consider installing solar panels or heat pumps to reduce dependence on grid electricity.
- Take advantage of government incentives like the **Smart Export Guarantee (SEG)** to earn money by selling excess energy back to the grid.

1.4. Smart Home Devices

- Install smart thermostats, LED lighting, and energy monitors to optimise energy usage.
- Savings: Smart thermostats can reduce heating bills by 10-15% annually.

2. Build an Emergency Fund

An emergency fund is a financial cushion that prevents you from relying on high-interest loans or credit cards during unexpected expenses.

2.1. Set a Savings Goal

- Aim to save 3-6 months' worth of living expenses.
- Start small: Even saving £10 a week adds up to £520 a year.

2.2. Automate Your Savings

- Set up a standing order to transfer a portion of your income to a savings account regularly.
- Use apps like *Moneybox* or *Plum* to round up purchases and save the spare change.

2.3. Use High-Interest Accounts

- Look for savings accounts or ISAs with competitive interest rates to grow your emergency fund faster.

3. Switch to Better Deals Regularly

The UK market is competitive for many services, from utilities to insurance. Regularly reviewing and switching can save you hundreds annually.

3.1. Utilities

- Use comparison sites like *Uswitch* and *MoneySuperMarket* to find the cheapest providers for energy, broadband, and mobile.

3.2. Insurance

- Never auto-renew car, home, or life insurance. Use platforms like *Confused.com* or *GoCompare* to compare quotes.

3.3. Subscriptions

- Review subscriptions annually and cancel any unused ones.

4. Optimise Debt Repayment

Debt can drain your finances with interest payments, but there are ways to manage it effectively.

4.1. Consolidate Debt

- Combine multiple debts into a single, lower-interest payment with a consolidation loan.

4.2. Use Balance Transfer Credit Cards

- Look for 0% interest balance transfer cards to temporarily pause interest charges and focus on reducing the principal amount.

4.3. Prioritise High-Interest Debt

- Pay off the most expensive debts (e.g., payday loans) first to reduce overall costs.

5. Create Additional Income Streams

Boosting your income can help you achieve financial goals faster.

5.1. Side Hustles

- Explore options like freelancing, tutoring, or selling handmade items on Etsy.

5.2. Rent Out Spare Space

- Rent a spare room through **Rent a Room Scheme**, which allows you to earn up to £7,500 tax-free annually.
- Use platforms like *Airbnb* for short-term rentals.

5.3. Invest in Dividend Stocks or Peer-to-Peer Lending

- Use platforms like *DividendMax* or *Ratesetter* to grow your savings passively.

6. Plan for Retirement

Ensuring you have sufficient funds for retirement is a critical long-term savings goal.

6.1. Maximise Pension Contributions

- Contribute to your workplace pension to take advantage of employer contributions and tax relief.

6.2. Open a Self-Invested Personal Pension (SIPP)

- If you're self-employed or want more control, consider opening a SIPP for additional retirement savings.

6.3. Delay State Pension

- Delaying your state pension can increase the amount you receive when you start claiming it.

7. Budget for Big Purchases

When planning major expenses like home improvements, a car, or a holiday, saving in advance reduces the need for costly credit.

7.1. Set a Goal and Timeline

- Break the cost into manageable monthly savings goals.

7.2. Use Savings Pots

- Apps like *Monzo* and *Starling Bank* let you create savings pots for specific goals.

Case Study: Emma's Long-Term Savings Success

Emma, a homeowner in Brighton, implemented several long-term savings strategies and reduced her overall expenses by £2,500 annually:

1. **Upgraded to Energy-Efficient Appliances**: Saved £150/year on electricity.

2. **Consolidated Debt**: Reduced monthly payments by £200 through a lower-interest loan.
3. **Switched Providers Regularly**: Saved £500/year by shopping around for energy, insurance, and broadband.
4. **Started a Side Hustle**: Earned £4,000/year by renting out her spare room.

Quick Wins for Long-Term Savings

1. Set up a direct debit for regular savings into a high-interest account.
2. Review energy and insurance providers annually for better deals.
3. Invest in energy-efficient home upgrades to reduce utility costs.
4. Use free budgeting tools like *YNAB* or *Emma* to track and optimise your finances.

Conclusion

Long-term savings strategies require patience and consistency, but the rewards are well worth the effort. By focusing on energy efficiency, building an emergency fund, optimising debt repayment, and creating additional income streams, you can secure your financial future. In the next chapter, we'll discuss free resources and tools available in the UK to help you save even more money on daily expenses.

Chapter 10: Free Resources and Tools to Save Money in the UK

In the UK, there are numerous free resources and tools designed to help households manage their finances, save money, and reduce expenses. Whether it's budgeting tools, cashback apps, or government schemes, these resources can make a significant impact on your savings. This chapter highlights the best free tools and programs to help you achieve your financial goals.

1. Budgeting and Expense Tracking

1.1. Budgeting Apps

- **Emma**: Tracks spending, highlights subscriptions, and provides insights into your financial habits.
- **Money Dashboard**: Links to your bank accounts to categorise expenses and monitor budgets.
- **Cleo**: A chatbot that analyses spending and offers budgeting tips in a fun, conversational way.

1.2. Spreadsheets

- Free budgeting templates are available online, such as *MoneySavingExpert's Budget Planner* or *Google Sheets* templates.

---

2. Cashback and Discount Apps

2.1. Cashback on Shopping

- **TopCashback**: Earn cashback when shopping online at thousands of retailers.
- **Quidco**: Similar to TopCashback, offering deals and cashback on everyday purchases.

2.2. Receipt Scanning Apps

- **Shoppix**: Upload receipts to earn points that can be redeemed for gift cards.
- **SnapMyEats**: Earn rewards for sharing photos of your food receipts.

2.3. Discount Shopping

- **Too Good To Go**: Get heavily discounted food from restaurants and supermarkets nearing their sell-by date.

- **Olio**: Share or pick up surplus food and household items for free in your local area.

---

3. Price Comparison Tools

3.1. Utilities and Insurance

- **Uswitch**: Compares energy, broadband, and mobile deals to find the cheapest options.
- **GoCompare**: Offers comparisons for insurance, utilities, and financial products.
- **Confused.com**: Ideal for car and home insurance comparisons.

3.2. Shopping

- **Trolley.co.uk**: Compares supermarket prices for groceries and household essentials.
- **PriceSpy**: Tracks price changes on products to ensure you're getting the best deal.

---

4. Free Entertainment and Education

4.1. Streaming and Audiobooks

- **BBC iPlayer**: Free streaming of UK TV shows, documentaries, and movies.
- **Libby** and **BorrowBox**: Borrow eBooks and audiobooks for free using your local library membership.

4.2. Fitness and Wellness

- **NHS Fitness Studio**: Free workout videos, from yoga to strength training.
- **FitOn**: Offers free workout plans and fitness programs.

4.3. Learning Platforms

- **FutureLearn**: Free online courses from UK universities.
- **Khan Academy**: Free educational videos and tutorials on various subjects.

5. Government Grants and Schemes

5.1. Home Energy

- **Warm Home Discount Scheme**: Provides a £150 discount on electricity bills for eligible households.
- **ECO4 Scheme**: Offers free or subsidised home improvements like insulation and heating upgrades.

5.2. Travel

- **Free Bus Pass for Seniors and Disabled**: Apply through your local council.
- **Cycle to Work Scheme**: Purchase a bike tax-free to save on commuting costs.

5.3. Childcare

- **Tax-Free Childcare**: For working parents, the government pays £2 for every £8 you contribute, up to £2,000/year per child.
- **15-30 Hours Free Childcare**: Available for children aged 3-4 in England.

6. Community Resources

6.1. Food Banks

- Organisations like **Trussell Trust** provide free food parcels to those in need.

6.2. Repair Cafes

- Attend local repair cafes where volunteers fix items like electronics, clothing, and bicycles for free.

6.3. Freecycle and Facebook Marketplace

- Platforms where people give away items they no longer need, from furniture to electronics.

---

7. Debt Management

7.1. Free Advice Services

- **StepChange Debt Charity**: Offers personalised debt advice and repayment plans.
- **National Debtline**: Provides free advice on managing debt and budgeting.

- **Citizens Advice**: Help with debt, benefits, and consumer rights.

7.2. Budgeting Help

- **CAP UK (Christians Against Poverty)**: Free budgeting courses and debt counselling.

---

8. Tools for Energy Savings

8.1. Smart Meters

- Offered free by energy suppliers to monitor real-time electricity and gas usage.

8.2. Energy-Saving Apps

- **Loop**: Tracks energy usage and identifies opportunities to save.
- **Samsung SmartThings Energy**: Helps optimise energy usage in smart appliances.

Case Study: Sophie's Savings with Free Resources

Sophie, a nurse in Bristol, reduced her expenses by £1,000/year using these tools:

1. **Cashback Apps**: Earned £200 through *TopCashback* and *Shoppix*.
2. **Energy Efficiency Tools**: Installed a free smart meter and used *Loop* to cut her electricity bill by 15%.
3. **Free Entertainment**: Borrowed audiobooks via *Libby* and streamed fitness classes from the NHS Fitness Studio.

Quick Wins with Free Resources

1. Use cashback apps for everyday purchases.
2. Borrow books and audiobooks through your local library.
3. Apply for government grants and schemes to reduce household costs.
4. Compare prices on utilities, insurance, and groceries to ensure you're not overpaying.

Conclusion

The UK offers a wealth of free resources and tools that can make saving money easier and more accessible. By leveraging these options, you can significantly reduce your expenses, increase your savings, and achieve greater financial stability. In the next chapter, we'll wrap up by summarising the key strategies covered in this book and providing a practical action plan to help you get started on your savings journey.

Chapter 11: Your Savings Action Plan

Congratulations on making it to the final chapter! Throughout this book, we've explored practical strategies to help you cut costs and manage your household expenses in the UK. Now, it's time to turn those strategies into action. This chapter will provide a step-by-step plan to help you implement the lessons you've learned and maximise your savings.

Step 1: Audit Your Finances

1. **Review Your Monthly Budget**
   - Use a budgeting tool like *Money Dashboard* or a spreadsheet to track your income and expenses.
   - Categorise your spending into essential (e.g., rent, bills) and non-essential (e.g., entertainment, subscriptions).
2. **Identify High-Cost Areas**
   - Highlight the top three expenses where you spend the most money (e.g., energy, groceries, transport).
   - Focus on these areas first to achieve the biggest impact.

Step 2: Quick Wins to Start Saving Today

1. **Switch Providers**
   - Use comparison sites like *Uswitch* to find better deals on energy, broadband, and insurance.
   - Contact your current providers and negotiate lower rates.
2. **Cancel Unused Subscriptions**
   - Review your bank statements for recurring payments.
   - Cancel subscriptions you don't use or replace them with free alternatives.
3. **Take Advantage of Free Resources**
   - Sign up for free cashback apps like *TopCashback* and *Shoppix*.
   - Use your local library for free books, audiobooks, and more.

Step 3: Plan for Long-Term Savings

1. **Set Up an Emergency Fund**
   - Start small, saving £10-£20 a week into a high-interest savings account or ISA.
   - Automate your savings to ensure consistency.
2. **Invest in Energy Efficiency**
   - Replace old appliances with energy-efficient models.
   - Apply for government grants like the ECO4 Scheme to insulate your home or upgrade your boiler.
3. **Pay Off High-Interest Debt**
   - Prioritise debts with the highest interest rates.
   - Consider consolidating debts or using a 0% balance transfer card to save on interest.

Step 4: Build Better Habits

1. **Plan Your Meals**
   - Create a weekly meal plan based on what you already have.
   - Shop with a list to avoid impulse purchases and reduce food waste.

2. **Monitor Your Usage**
    - Install a smart meter to track energy usage and identify wasteful habits.
    - Use apps like *Loop* or *Samsung SmartThings Energy* to monitor and optimise your consumption.
3. **Use Public Transport Wisely**
    - Invest in railcards or season tickets for regular travel.
    - Travel off-peak to save on fares.

Step 5: Maximise Your Income

1. **Explore Side Hustles**
    - Offer freelance services, sell handmade products, or tutor online to generate extra income.
    - Use platforms like *Etsy*, *Upwork*, or *TaskRabbit*.
2. **Rent Out Space**
    - Rent a spare room through the Rent a Room Scheme to earn up to £7,500 tax-free.
    - Use *Airbnb* for short-term lets.

3. **Take Advantage of Tax Relief**
   - Check for available tax credits or deductions based on your circumstances, such as working-from-home expenses.

Step 6: Stay Organised

1. **Set Reminders for Renewals**
   - Use your calendar or apps like Cleo to track subscription and contract renewal dates.
   - Avoid auto-renewals by negotiating or switching to better deals.
2. **Review Your Budget Regularly**
   - Reassess your spending every three months to ensure you're staying on track.
3. **Celebrate Small Wins**
   - Reward yourself for hitting savings milestones to stay motivated.

Example Action Plan: First Month

Week	Action	Estimated Savings
Week 1	Review your budget and highlight unnecessary expenses.	£50
Week 2	Cancel unused subscriptions and switch energy/broadband providers.	£100
Week 3	Start meal planning and use cashback apps for grocery shopping.	£20
Week 4	Apply for government schemes (e.g., Warm Home Discount) and railcards.	£150
Total		£320

Slash Your Bills: A Practical Guide to Saving Money in the UK 2025

Case Study: John's Transformation

John, a 35-year-old teacher in Birmingham, implemented this action plan:

1. **Switched Providers**: Saved £150/year on energy and £80/year on broadband.
2. **Cut Subscriptions**: Cancelled unused streaming services, saving £25/month.
3. **Meal Planned**: Reduced grocery spending by £30/month through careful planning.
4. **Invested in Insulation**: Took advantage of the ECO4 Scheme to insulate his home, reducing heating bills by 20%.

Total Annual Savings: £1,000+

Quick Tips for Success

1. Start small: Focus on one category of expenses at a time.
2. Automate your savings: Set up direct debits to save without thinking about it.
3. Stay informed: Follow *MoneySavingExpert* or similar sites for ongoing tips and deals.

Conclusion

Saving money doesn't have to feel overwhelming. By taking small, consistent steps and using the strategies outlined in this book, you can regain control of your finances and work toward your long-term goals. Start with the quick wins, plan for the future, and watch your savings grow. Remember, every pound saved is a step closer to financial freedom.

Good luck on your savings journey!

To effectively manage your household expenses and meal planning, utilising printable trackers can be highly beneficial. Here are some free resources tailored for UK households:

1. Monthly Bill Trackers

Keeping track of your bills ensures timely payments and helps avoid late fees. Here are some printable bill trackers:

- **Printabulls' Monthly Bill Organisers**: Offers 18 unique templates to monitor bill due dates and amounts.

  www.printabulls.com

- **World of Printables' Bill Tracker**: A simple template to log bill details, due dates, and payment status.

  www.worldofprintables.com

- **Money Saving Central's Monthly Budget Planner**: Helps in planning monthly income and expenses across various categories.

  www.moneysavingcentral.co.uk

2. Meal Planner Templates

Organising your meals can lead to healthier eating habits and reduced food waste. Consider these meal planner templates:

- **Canva's Free Printable Meal Planner Templates**: Customisable designs to plan weekly meals, available in various styles.

    www.canva.com/planners

- **British Nutrition Foundation's Weekly Meal Planner**: A straightforward template to schedule meals and snacks throughout the week.

    www.nutrition.org.uk

- **Liana's Kitchen Meal Planner Template**: Assists in organising meals and creating shopping lists to save on food bills.

    www.lianaskitchen.co.uk

3. Comprehensive Budget Planners

For an all-encompassing approach to budgeting, these planners can be useful:

- **Printabulls' Monthly Budget Planners**: Provides 20 free printable templates to plan monthly income and expenses.

    www.printabulls.com

- **101 Planners' Budget Sheet Template**: Editable templates in various formats to calculate monthly expenses and income.

    www.101planners.com

These resources can assist you in effectively managing your household expenses and meal planning. Choose the templates that best fit your needs, print them out, and incorporate them into your daily routine to enhance your financial and meal planning strategies.

www.ingramcontent.com/pod-product-compliance
Lightning Source LLC
Chambersburg PA
CBHW071412220526
45469CB00004B/1265